INSIDE

GPS

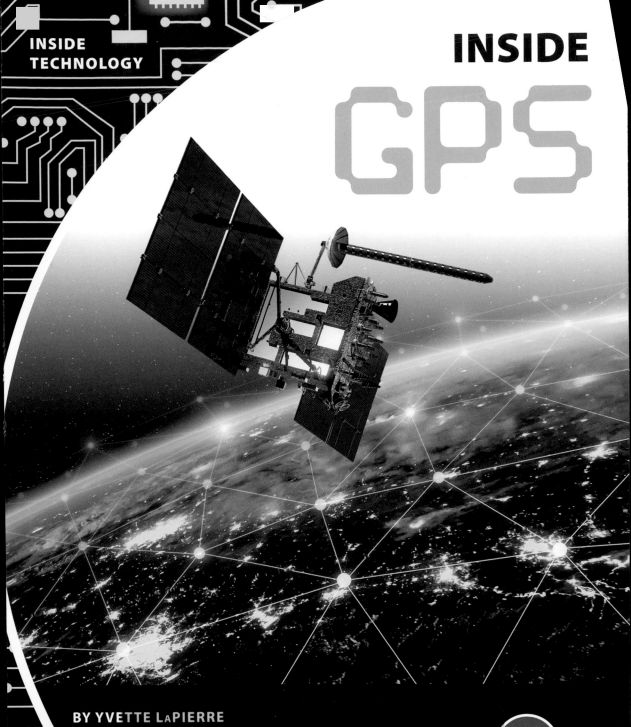

BY YVETTE LaPIERRE

CONTENT CONSULTANT
Dennis Akos, PhD
Professor, Colorado Center for Astrodynamics Research
University of Colorado

Cover image
receiver

Core Library

An Imprint of Abdo Publishing
abdobooks.com

abdocorelibrary.com

Published by Abdo Publishing, a division of ABDO, PO Box 398166, Minneapolis, Minnesota 55439. Copyright © 2019 by Abdo Consulting Group, Inc. International copyrights reserved in all countries. No part of this book may be reproduced in any form without written permission from the publisher. Core Library™ is a trademark and logo of Abdo Publishing.

Printed in the United States of America, North Mankato, Minnesota
092018
012019

THIS BOOK CONTAINS
RECYCLED MATERIALS

Cover Photos: Shutterstock Images, foreground, background
Interior Photos: Shutterstock Images, 1 (foreground), 1 (background); iStockphoto, 4–5, 29, 32 (front); United Launch Alliance/US Air Force, 7, 12–13, 43; RA Photos/iStockphoto, 10; United States Government, 16, 17, 22–23, 45; Andy Cross/The Denver Post/Getty Images, 18–19; Science & Society Picture Library/Getty Images, 24; Ratib Al Safadi/Anadolu Agency/Getty Images, 26–27; Airman 1st Class Perry Aston/US Air Force, 31; Johnson Space Center/NASA, 32 (back); Ashley Cooper/Construction Photography/Avalon/Hulton Archive/Getty Images, 34–35; AB Forces News Collection/Alamy, 39

Editor: Megan Ellis
Series Designer: Ryan Gale

Library of Congress Control Number: 2018949773

Publisher's Cataloging-in-Publication Data

Names: LaPierre, Yvette, author.
Title: Inside GPS / by Yvette LaPierre.
Description: Minneapolis, Minnesota : Abdo Publishing, 2019 | Series: Inside technology | Includes online resources and index.
Identifiers: ISBN 9781532117923 (lib. bdg.) | ISBN 9781641856171 (pbk) | ISBN 9781532170782 (ebook)
Subjects: LCSH: Technological innovations--Juvenile literature. | Global Positioning System--Juvenile literature. | Global Positioning System--Maps--Juvenile literature.
Classification: DDC 526.6--dc23

CONTENTS

WORLDWIDE NAVIGATION

Anthony is lost. He has been driving for hours but can't find his friend's new house. He drives into a gas station and puts the car in park. He then turns on a car app that uses the Global Positioning System (GPS). Anthony enters the street address. A map appears onscreen. The GPS receiver locates his car on the map. Then the map shows the house Anthony is looking for. As he drives, the car's location changes on the map. The GPS shows his car on the map. Soon, Anthony arrives at the house, thanks to GPS satellites thousands of miles overhead.

The GPS unit and map in a car can help someone find his or her way around.

ACCESS FOR ALL

At first the GPS signals that civilians could use were not very good. The US government made the civilian satellite signals less accurate than the military ones. This is called selective availability. The readings could be wrong by as much as a football field. The government did this on purpose. It wanted the military to have an advantage. The government worried that enemies could use GPS technology against the United States.

Eventually the US government realized the importance of accurate GPS for everyone. It stopped the selective availability in 2000. Public GPS became up to ten times better. Today, anyone with a receiver has access to free and accurate signals.

GPS is a worldwide navigation system that uses satellites. The satellites send signals to receivers. A receiver uses these signals to determine its exact location. This ability to track location has many helpful uses.

GPS FOR EVERYONE

GPS was invented by the US military. The first satellite was launched in 1978. GPS was designed for both civilians and the military to use. At first, GPS was only used

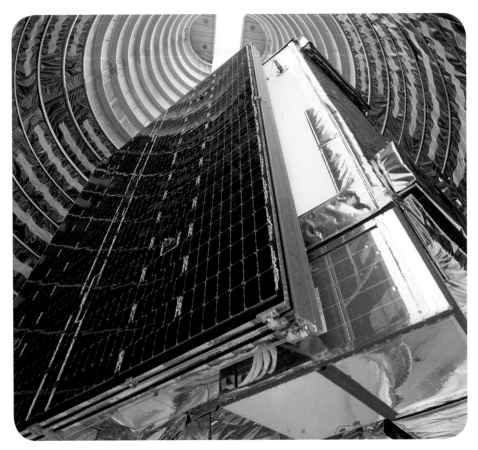

GPS satellites are built on the ground before being launched into space.

by the military. It guided rockets and missiles to their targets. It helped ships navigate and tracked troops on the ground. Soldiers used GPS to find their way around new places.

GPS was made available for public use in 1983. The military still uses it. But now more than 3 billion people around the world use GPS.

TRANSPORTATION

Many people use GPS to help them find their way around. Delivery drivers use GPS to locate addresses. Trucking companies install GPS units to track their trucks. This is how customers can find out when their packages will be delivered. GPS can be used to monitor traffic on roads. This can help prevent traffic jams and accidents.

Pilots also use GPS. GPS units can tell where a plane is at any part of its flight. It can help pilots know the location of nearby planes. GPS can even help pilots land planes when bad weather makes it hard to see. GPS helps make car and airplane travel safer. It is also more reliable than paper maps. It can even save lives.

Ambulances and other emergency vehicles use GPS. It helps emergency responders reach the scene of an accident or disaster. GPS helps search and rescue efforts find people in trouble.

BUSINESS AND FUN

Many businesses are helped by GPS. Farmers use GPS to plant and manage their crops. GPS helps miners, construction workers, and road surveyors do their jobs. Scientists use GPS to track wildlife, find changes to the land, and predict earthquakes. Banks and power companies rely on the accurate time data provided by GPS.

GPS can be used for fun, too. Hikers use

RIVAL SYSTEMS

GPS is not the only satellite navigation system. Some other countries have global systems, too. Most other countries call satellite navigation systems Global Navigation Satellite Systems (GNSS). The Soviet Union began using a GNSS in 1982. It is called GLONASS. It has 24 satellites. The Soviet Union later broke up into several countries. The largest, Russia, continues to operate GLONASS today.

Europe is building a 30-satellite system called Galileo. It's due to be finished in 2020. China is also building a GNSS. It's called the BeiDou Navigation Satellite System. BeiDou comes from the Chinese name for the Big Dipper constellation, *Běidǒuxīng*. The Big Dipper was often used for navigation before GPS and compasses existed.

A geocache can be found using a GPS unit. It may have a logbook or souvenirs inside.

GPS to explore new places. Runners and bikers use it to track their routes. Geocachers hunt for hidden clues following GPS directions. Apps that use GPS can show people restaurants nearby.

GPS has become part of everyday life. Today, people and places can be located anywhere on the planet using GPS technology. For example, map databases such as Google Maps use GPS and user information to provide directions and traffic information. A network of satellites, ground stations, and receivers makes this possible.

STRAIGHT TO THE
SOURCE

The website GPS.gov provides official government information about GPS. In an article titled "Public Safety & Disaster Relief," it mentions how important GPS is for first responders. According to the article:

Knowing the precise location of landmarks, streets, buildings, emergency service resources, and disaster relief sites . . . saves lives. This information is critical to disaster relief teams. . . . GPS has played a vital role in relief efforts for global disasters such as the tsunami that struck in the Indian Ocean region in 2004, Hurricanes Katrina and Rita that wreaked havoc in the Gulf of Mexico in 2005, and the Pakistan-Indian earthquake in 2005. Search and rescue teams used GPS . . . to create maps of the disaster areas for rescue and aid operations, as well as to assess damage.

Source: National Coordination Office for Space-Based Positioning, Navigation, and Timing. "Public Safety & Disaster Relief." *GPS.gov*. GPS.gov, 2006. Web. Accessed June 19, 2018.

Back It Up

The article is using evidence to support a point. Write a paragraph describing the point the article is making. What are two or three pieces of evidence the article uses to make the point?

SATELLITES IN THE SKY

Hundreds of years ago, people used the positions of stars to help them get around. Now people use satellites in space. More than 30 GPS satellites orbit Earth. At least 24 are working at any time. The rest are spares in case a satellite needs to be fixed.

A rocket motor launches the satellite into space. Satellites also have smaller motors, or thrusters. Thrusters adjust the satellite when it drifts out of position in the orbit. Satellites have a metal body strong enough to survive the launch into space. It is called a bus. The bus holds the satellite together.

In 2015, the US Air Force used Delta IV rockets to launch upgraded GPS satellites into space.

Each satellite weighs 2,000 to 4,000 pounds (900 to 1,800 kg). They are about 17 feet (5.2 m) long. This includes their solar panels. They extend like wings. They turn sunlight into electricity which is stored in rechargeable batteries or fuel cells. On-board computers control the satellite. The satellites also have antennas that send signals to receivers on Earth.

SPEED AND GRAVITY

GPS satellites are launched into space on rockets. Once in space, the satellites travel around Earth. Gravity keeps them in orbit. The satellite's speed sends it up into space. The force of gravity pulls the satellite back toward Earth. If the satellite is going too fast, it will fly off into space in a straight line. If the speed is too slow, gravity will pull it crashing back to Earth. When the speed of the satellite is balanced by the pull of gravity, the satellite stays in orbit around Earth.

SATELLITES IN ORBIT

GPS satellites orbit around Earth. This means they move around Earth in space. But they do not fly away. They are held in place by the planet's gravity.

The satellites are approximately 12,550 miles (20,200 km) above the surface of Earth. They travel approximately 8,700 miles per hour (14,000 km/h). One complete orbit takes 12 hours. This means each satellite makes two trips around the planet every day.

Objects in orbit follow an imaginary flat surface, or plane. The shape of the orbit is an ellipse. An ellipse is similar to an oval.

Satellites are arranged into six orbital planes around Earth. There is room for 27 working satellites. Together, these orbital planes are called the GPS constellation.

SPEED OF LIGHT

Satellite signals travel at the speed of light. The speed of light is constant. It is about 186,000 miles (300,000 km) per second. GPS receivers use the amount of time it takes a signal to travel to Earth to help calculate the distance. But Earth's upper atmosphere contains charged particles. Weather occurs in the lower atmosphere. These factors can distort and delay signals. GPS receivers must correct for these differences.

ORBITAL PLANES

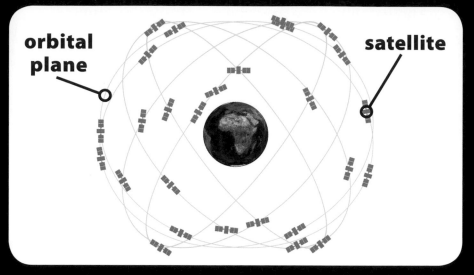

orbital plane

satellite

The six orbital planes surround Earth. The planes are spaced equally. The satellites stay in their orbital planes. This arrangement covers the planet. Take a look at the diagram. How can people on Earth view multiple satellites at once? Why do some of the orbital planes overlap?

SENDING MESSAGES

Each satellite sends signals down to Earth. The signals are sent as radio waves. They are sent constantly. The radio signals travel at the speed of light. Each signal gives several pieces of information about the satellite.

First, it identifies which satellite sent the signal. Next, the signal has information about the health of the satellite. It also gives the location of the satellite

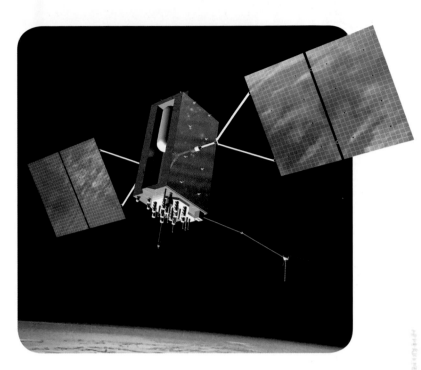

Satellites such as this GPS III satellite send messages to receivers on Earth.

in orbit. The signal then gives the exact time the signal was sent. The signals are sent to special receivers on the ground called monitoring stations.

Each satellite sends signals at the exact same time. The time is kept by a very accurate clock on board the satellite called an atomic clock. Atomic clocks must be precise. One nanosecond is equal to one billionth of a second. An error of one nanosecond means the data from a GPS satellite will be off by one foot (30 cm).

STATIONS ON EARTH

Ground control stations track and control satellites. They correct for errors. This helps GPS navigation be as accurate as possible. The ground facilities include monitor stations, a master control station, and ground antennas. The facilities are spread around the world.

MONITOR STATIONS

There are 16 GPS monitoring sites. The stations monitor the location, speed, and overall health of the satellites. They also make sure the atomic clocks are on time. Each station checks up on satellites twice a day.

The master control station is located in Colorado Springs, Colorado. Its antennas help monitor GPS satellites all over the world.

The stations also collect data about the atmosphere. Parts of Earth's atmosphere can distort the satellite's signals. Other obstacles can get in the way of a clear signal. These include trees and tall buildings. The monitor stations send all this information to the master control station.

MASTER CONTROL STATION

The master control station oversees the entire GPS constellation. US Air Force operators staff the control station 24 hours a day, seven days a week. The operators are nicknamed Team Blackjack. They use the data sent

CONTROL LOCATIONS

There are many GPS ground stations. They help detect problems in GPS quickly and accurately. The master control station is in Colorado Springs, Colorado. There is an alternate master control station. It is located on an Air Force base in California. There are monitoring stations as far north as Greenland and as far south as New Zealand. Stations and antennas are found on every continent except Antarctica.

from the monitor stations to determine the exact location of each satellite. They analyze the data and look for problems. For example, the gravity of the sun and the moon pulls on the satellites. This can change a satellite's orbit.

The master control station operators also monitor the atomic clocks. They make sure the clocks on each satellite are keeping the correct time.

MEASURING EARTHQUAKES

Scientists from the United States Geological Survey (USGS) use GPS to measure earthquake activity. They place GPS receivers in the ground near earthquake faults. The receivers can detect ground movement as small as five millimeters. Movements that small normally can't be detected. Scientists are researching whether these small-scale movements predict where and when an earthquake will happen.

Scientists also use the GPS receivers to measure the strength of an earthquake quickly. They can then predict whether dangerous ocean waves will result. GPS helps scientists better understand earthquakes, which can save lives.

Team Blackjack operators monitor GPS satellites using many computers.

Accurate GPS navigation needs the precise location of satellites and the exact timing of signals. If the operators find a problem, they create messages to fix the problem. The next step is to get the messages to the satellites.

GROUND ANTENNAS

The ground antennas are the messengers. The antennas send the messages from the master control station to the satellites. These messages keep the GPS satellites

The first accurate atomic clock was the caesium atomic clock. It was built in 1955.

working correctly. A message might contain directions to correct a satellite's atomic clock. Or it might have a command to change the satellite's orbit. The command tells the satellite's thruster rockets to fire and nudge the satellite back into the correct orbit. The antennas can send information to satellites up to three times a day.

ATOMIC TIME

An atomic clock is one of the most accurate timepieces ever. It loses only one second in up to 100 million years. Atomic clocks measure the precise length of a second. A second is the basic unit of timekeeping. All clocks track the passage of time with each "tick" of a second.

A grandfather clock has a pendulum. It swings about once per second. GPS atomic clocks don't use swinging pendulums. Instead, they use vibrating atoms. Atoms vibrate an exact number of times per second. Atomic clocks keep track of time by counting the atomic vibrations.

EXPLORE ONLINE

Chapter Three discusses the operation of the master control station by Team Blackjack. The video at the website below goes into more depth on this topic. Does it help you understand how Team Blackjack maintains the GPS constellation?

2 SOPS KEEPS GPS FLYING!
abdocorelibrary.com/inside-GPS

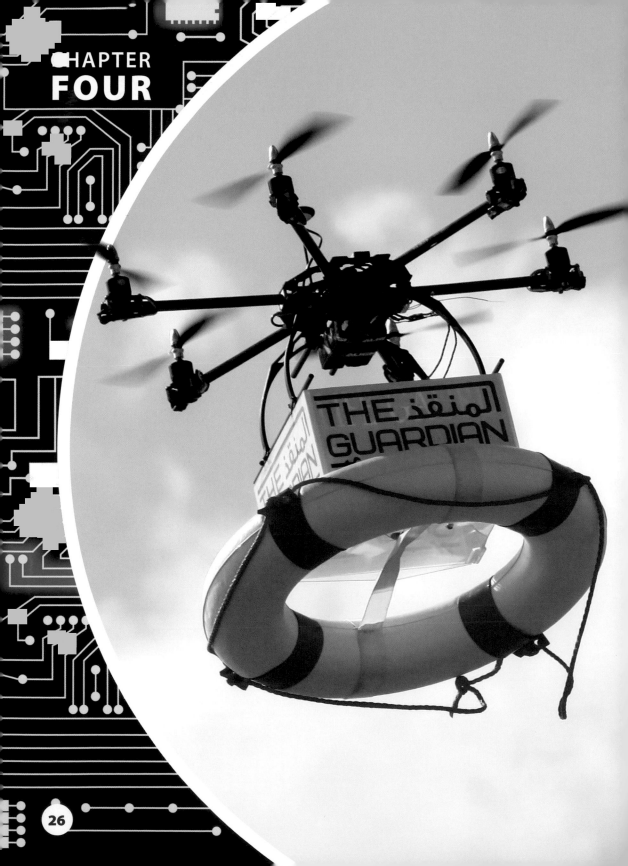

RECEIVERS IN HAND

Signals are continuously sent from GPS satellites. Ground stations detect errors in the signals. They send corrections back up to the satellites. GPS receivers pick up the accurate satellite signals. They use information from the signal to determine location.

There are many types of receivers. Small receivers are built into many smartphones and laptop computers. Receivers can be small enough to fit inside a GPS smartwatch. Handheld GPS receivers help hikers explore new trails. These receivers have batteries that

First responders can use GPS receivers in remote controllers to pilot drones. These drones can help them rescue people who are injured.

27

can run for several hours. Many new cars have larger GPS receivers in the dashboard. The largest receivers are used in commercial airplanes and large military vehicles. All receivers help people know where they are.

GATHERING SIGNALS

A GPS receiver picks up a satellite signal. It gathers important data. The signal identifies which satellite sent the data as well as the location of the satellite at the time the signal was sent. It tells the precise time the signal

MEASURING CLIMATE CHANGE

Scientists use GPS for climate change research. Greenland has a sheet of ice that is thousands of feet thick. It sits on top of bedrock. The ice is so heavy, it pushes the rock down. As Earth warms, the ice melts. The ice sheet becomes lighter. There is less to push down on the bedrock. The bedrock rises slightly. A GPS receiver on the sheet of ice tracks the movement. It can tell how high the bedrock rises.

Hikers can use GPS to find their way even when there aren't roads or trails.

RELATIVE CLOCKS

Time flows slightly faster on GPS satellites than it does on the ground. That's due to the theories of special and general relativity. Physicist Albert Einstein proposed these theories. Special relativity says time speeds up or slows down depending on how fast something is moving in relation to something else. General relativity predicts that strong gravity makes time move slower.

Atomic clocks on board satellites appear to be ticking faster than clocks on Earth. They gain about 38 microseconds a day. That is what a calculation using the two theories predicts. GPS receivers correct for this difference in time.

left the satellite. The receiver also notes the exact time it received the signal.

The receiver uses this information to figure out how far it is from the satellite. It uses this formula: distance = rate x time. Rate is the speed of light. All radio signals travel at this speed. Time is the difference between when the signal left the satellite and when it was received. The receiver multiplies rate and time. Then it knows the distance to the satellite.

The receiver needs to locate four or more satellites. It calculates its distance to each satellite. It uses that information to determine its location. The more satellites the device uses, the more precise the location.

GPS GEOMETRY

Geometry is math that uses shapes, like lines, circles, and triangles. Receivers use this type of math to calculate their location. Think of satellite signals as flashlights. If someone shines a flashlight from up high, a circle of light appears on the ground. The receiver doesn't know exactly where it is in relation to the flashlight. But it knows it is somewhere in that circle

TRILATERATION

GPS is made up of three parts: satellites, ground stations, and receivers. These parts use four GPS satellites to trilaterate location. Trilateration helps determine location using geometry and shapes such as circles and triangles. Three of the satellites help solve the position of something. The fourth satellite is used to account for any errors in the clock of the receiver. Take a look at the diagram below. How do these parts work together to make GPS work? What would happen if one of the parts wasn't working?

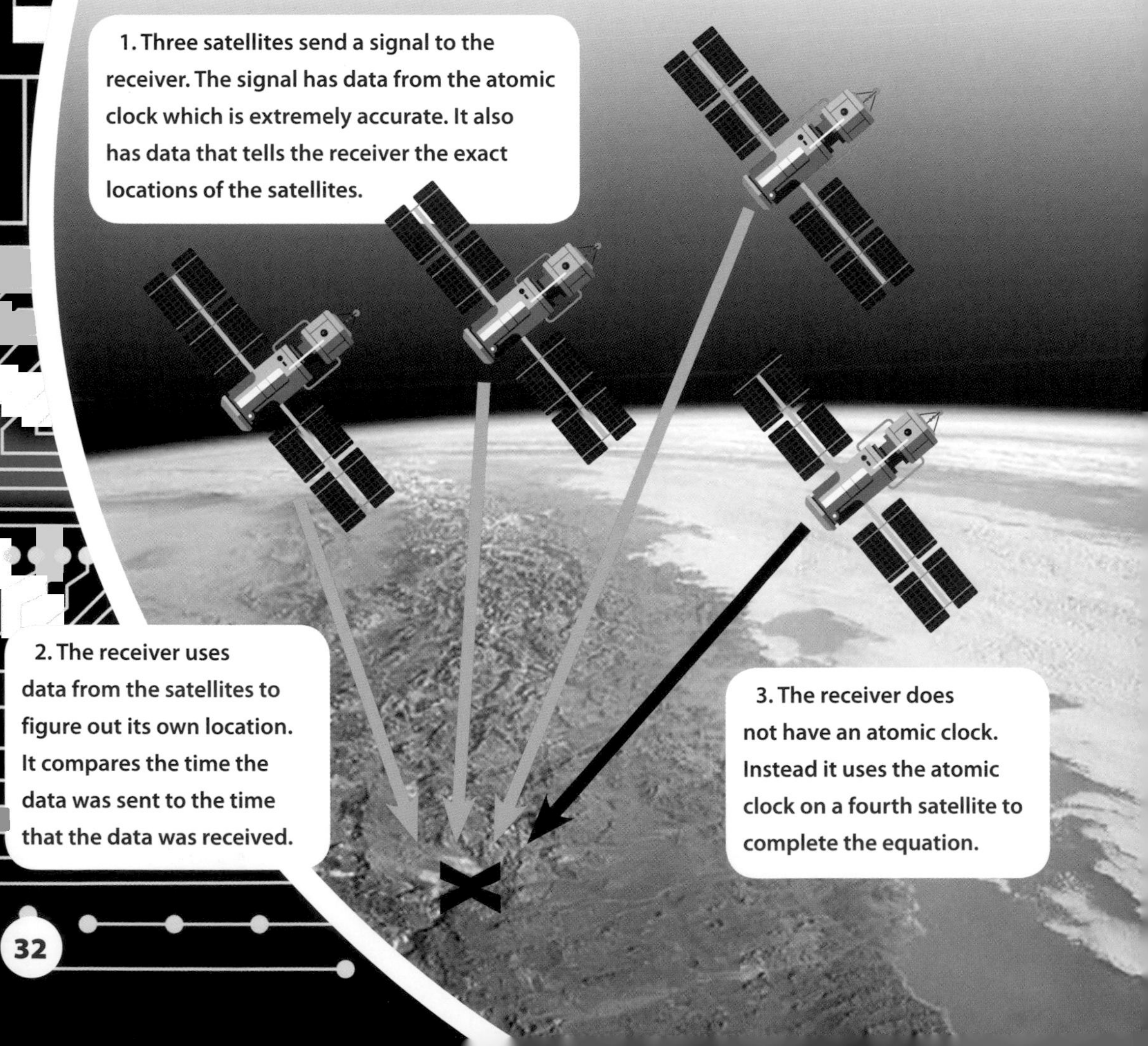

1. Three satellites send a signal to the receiver. The signal has data from the atomic clock which is extremely accurate. It also has data that tells the receiver the exact locations of the satellites.

2. The receiver uses data from the satellites to figure out its own location. It compares the time the data was sent to the time that the data was received.

3. The receiver does not have an atomic clock. Instead it uses the atomic clock on a fourth satellite to complete the equation.

of light. Now three more flashlights beam circles of light on the ground. Those four circles intersect at one point only. That is the exact location of the receiver.

Receivers use an advanced form of this calculation. Instead of flat circles, the signal shapes are spheres. A sphere is a three-dimensional circle, like a ball. The receiver finds its position in three dimensions. The three dimensions are latitude, longitude, and altitude.

FURTHER EVIDENCE

Chapter Four explains how a GPS receiver uses math to find its location. What was one of the main points of this chapter? What key evidence supports this point? Take a look at the article about GPS receivers below. Find a quote from the website that supports the chapter's main point.

NASA SCIFILES
abdocorelibrary.com/inside-GPS

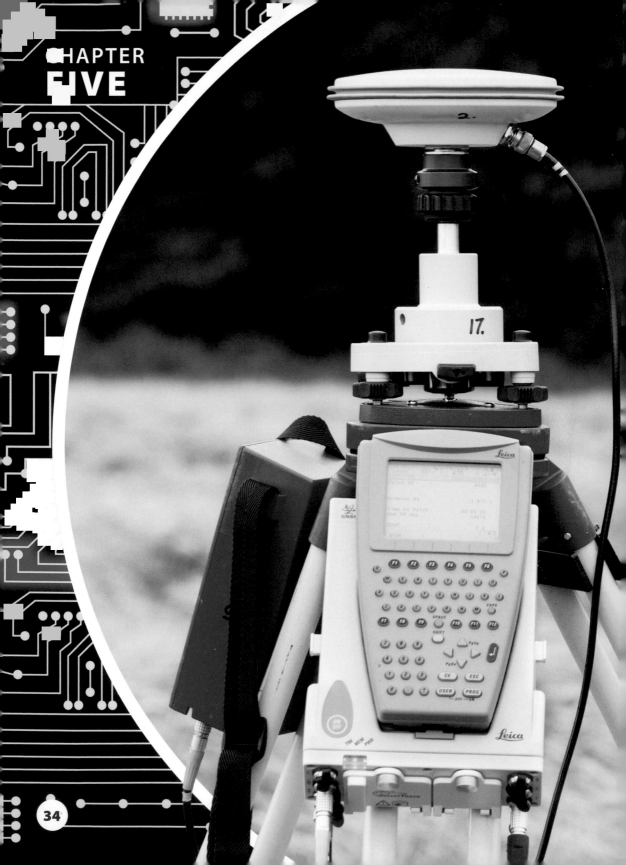

THE FUTURE OF GPS

GPS technology is accurate and reliable. Users can find their way to most places on the planet. But GPS isn't perfect. Obstacles get in the way of signals. Engineers are working to overcome problems. The US government is committed to making GPS even better. The more accurate GPS is, the more ways it can be used.

DIFFERENTIAL GPS

Sometimes tall objects get in the way of signals. For example, a satellite signal can bounce off a tall building. That makes the receiver think the satellite is farther away than

Differential GPS uses two receivers. One is stationary and the other moves around.

SPOOFERS AND JAMMERS

Researchers are working to make GPS safe from attacks. There are two types of attacks experts worry about. They are called spoofing and jamming. Spoofing is when someone sends a false GPS signal. It is slightly stronger than a real GPS signal. If a car GPS system picked up a spoofed signal, it could send the driver in the wrong direction. This could cause cars or airplanes to crash into objects.

GPS jammers block out GPS signals entirely. Jammers can knock out mobile phone service. They can disrupt GPS used by emergency vehicles and airlines. GPS jammers and spoofers are illegal in the United States.

it really is. Sometimes a satellite sends bad data. It may send the wrong time or position. A receiver needs correct information to calculate the right location.

Technology called Differential GPS (DGPS) corrects for these errors. DGPS hardware is installed in a stationary receiver. The DGPS knows its exact location, which never changes. It can tell when it receives a GPS signal with an inaccurate location. The station sends a message to all DGPS receivers in the area with the corrected information. In the future, DGPS will help keep satellites and receivers more accurate.

IMPROVING GPS

The US government has a program to modernize GPS. It is spending billions of dollars to make GPS perform better. It also will make GPS more secure against possible attacks. GPS contains a mix of old and new satellites. The US will continue to replace old satellites with new and better ones.

A main focus of the program is to improve civilian GPS. Currently, military GPS sends signals on two channels. Civilian GPS uses only one channel. That means military GPS is slightly better. The government is adding three new signals for civilian use. That will make civilian GPS more accurate. The US government is also adding the civilian signals to new satellites as they replace old ones. These signals will be used for aviation and emergency services.

SPACE NAVIGATION

GPS can direct spacecraft to the moon, but no farther. Signals from satellites don't reach deep into space. That's because GPS satellites face Earth. The system is designed with the satellites in a low orbit around Earth. But scientists are working on a galactic positioning system. This space navigation system won't use satellites. Instead, it may be able to navigate by pulsars. Pulsars are a type of star that blinks on and off at precise intervals.

FUTURE RECEIVERS

Most receivers used today receive signals on one radio frequency. These receivers work well for most people's daily use. But single-frequency receivers aren't accurate enough for all uses, such as surveying land or exploring for oil deep underground.

New receivers can use two signal frequencies. Dual-frequency receivers can correct for errors. They are more accurate, even underground or surrounded by obstacles like tall trees.

Technicians prepare to send the new-and-improved GPS IIF-series satellite to space.

Better satellites, signals, and receivers are opening up new uses for GPS. For example, a car with an accurate GPS and map database would know exactly where it was at all times. It would know where the road was. By using a radar or shared GPS information from other cars on the road, the car would even know where nearby cars were. If that information could be fed to a computer that controls the car, the car wouldn't need a driver. The GPS system is one of the features that would allow the car to drive itself.

Today, people with receivers can locate themselves anywhere on the planet using GPS for free. GPS keeps roads and skyways safer by guiding cars and planes. It can even make sure that a drone delivers a package safely to someone's doorstep. New uses for GPS are invented daily. A satellite navigation system may soon guide us to deep space and almost anywhere our imaginations take us.

STRAIGHT TO THE
SOURCE

Greg Milner is the author of the book *Pinpoint: How GPS is Changing Technology, Culture, and Our Minds.* In the book, Milner describes some of the consequences of the success of GPS:

> *It is difficult to imagine life without [GPS], and so quickly that we are just beginning to confront the possible consequences. A single GPS timing flaw, whether accidental or maliciously installed, could bring down the electrical grid, hijack drones, or halt the world financial system. We now trust our devices so much that we follow them blindly down abandoned roads, over cliffs, and into the ocean; park rangers call this "death by GPS."*

> Source: Greg Milner. *Pinpoint: How GPS is Changing Technology, Culture, and Our Minds.* New York: W. W. Norton & Company, 2016. Print. 20.

Changing Minds

This text passage argues that we may depend on GPS too much. Do you agree that relying on GPS is dangerous? Write a short essay trying to change your friend's mind. Make sure you detail your opinion and your reasons for it. Include facts and details that support your opinion.

FAST FACTS

- GPS stands for Global Positioning System.

- The first GPS satellite was launched in 1978.

- GPS was originally designed for military use. It was made public in 1983 but was intentionally made less accurate than the military version. In 2000, the signal was improved for civilians.

- Transportation is the main use for GPS. Cars, aircraft, and other vehicles use GPS to navigate from place to place.

- GPS is made up of satellites, ground stations, and receivers.

- GPS satellites orbit about 12,550 miles (20,200 km) high. They orbit Earth every 12 hours.

- GPS satellites continuously send signals with information about the satellite's location and accurate time.

- Ground stations include monitor stations, ground antennas, and a master control station. They track and control satellites and correct signal errors.

- A receiver uses signals from four satellites to calculate its position.

- The US government is spending billions of dollars to modernize GPS to make it faster and even more accurate.

- Researchers are working on GPS technologies that will work indoors, underground, and in deep space.

STOP AND
THINK

Dig Deeper

After reading this book, what questions do you still have about GPS? With an adult's help, find a few reliable sources that can help you answer your questions. Write a paragraph about what you learned.

Why Do I Care?

Maybe you have never used a GPS receiver yourself. But that doesn't mean you can't think about how GPS helps people get around. Do your friends and family use GPS receivers? How might your life be different without GPS?

Another View

Chapter One discusses how GPS signals were limited to military use until 2000. As you know, every source is different. Ask a librarian or another adult to help you find another source about the beginning of GPS. Write a short essay comparing the new source's point of view with that of this book's author. How are they similar and why? How are they different and why?

You Are There

This book describes GPS satellites and how they orbit Earth. Imagine you are on a GPS satellite. Write a letter telling your friends about it. What do you notice about the satellite and how it moves? Be sure to add plenty of detail to your letter.

GLOSSARY

atmosphere
the mixture of gases that surrounds Earth or another planet

civilian
a person or something related to people who are not part of the military

drone
an aircraft without a pilot that is controlled remotely

galactic
relating to a galaxy such as the Milky Way

gravity
the force that pulls things toward the center of Earth

latitude
the distance north or south of the equator

longitude
the distance east or west of an imaginary line that runs through Greenwich, England

navigation
the science of determining location and plotting a course to a destination

precise
very accurate

relative
having meaning or truth only in relation to something else

three-dimensional
having the three dimensions of length, width, and height

thrusters
small rockets on a satellite that can change the satellite's flight path

ONLINE RESOURCES

To learn more about GPS, visit our free resource websites below.

Core Library
CONNECTION
FREE! COMMON CORE MULTIMEDIA RESOURCES

Visit **abdocorelibrary.com** for free Common Core resources for teachers and students, including vetted activities, multimedia, and booklinks, for deeper subject comprehension.

Booklinks
NONFICTION NETWORK
FREE! ONLINE NONFICTION RESOURCES

Visit **abdobooklinks.com** for free additional online weblinks for further learning. These links are routinely monitored and updated to provide the most current information available.

LEARN MORE

Kaul, Jennifer. *Inside Smartphones.* Minneapolis, MN: Abdo, 2019.

Panchyk, Richard. *Charting the World.* Chicago, IL: Chicago Review Press, 2011.

INDEX

About the Author

Yvette LaPierre lives in North Dakota with her family, two dogs, and two crested geckos. She likes to travel and uses GPS when she drives to new cities.